sundance
publishing

LITTLE RED
READERS

The School Bus Ride

**PETER SLOAN &
SHERYL SLOAN**

Illustrated by Gali Weiss.

Early in the morning,
the McIvor children
get on the school bus.
It starts from their house
on the hill.
Mrs. McIvor is the driver.

First the bus stops
at a cabin in the forest.
The Wood children get on.
"Good morning,
Mrs. McIvor the driver,"
they say.

Next the bus stops
at a house by the lake.
The Waters children get on.
"Good morning,
Mrs. McIvor the driver,"
they say.

4

Then the bus stops
at a lighthouse by the sea.
The Beach children get on.
"Good morning,
Mrs. McIvor the driver,"
they say.

After that the bus stops
at a farmhouse.
The Hay children get on.
"Good morning,
Mrs. McIvor the driver,"
they say.

Finally the bus stops
at a houseboat.
The Banks children get on.
"Good morning,
Mrs. McIvor the driver,"
they say.

When the children arrive
at school, they are happy.
They have had
a good ride.
"See you after school,
Mrs. McIvor the driver,"
they say.